Dad

I want to say, no shout out loud
Of our Dad I am so proud,
He said I was a truthful Son,
His very own George Washington.

At Christmas time he sang a lot,
'The Little Boy that Santa forgot'
He always made sure we had toys,
We were such very lucky Boys.

That little Boy he had no Dad,
And that would always make me sad,
Especially when I found out,
It was my Dad Nat sang about.

When I was eight I had a scare,
It was a frightening Nightmare,
I ran to be my Dads side,
And told him that I dreamt he died.

He told me, no he did swear,
He wasn't going anywhere,
He kept that promise till Eighty Three,
When came along the dreaded 'C'.

He fought that monster like a Man,
At least as well as any can,

He lived his life like many would,
Tried to enjoy it all he could.

He didn't always get it right,
But it was a challenge to win that fight,
Contrary he was but would not admit,
If wrong on a point he would not submit.

He wasn't perfect all the time,
But he'd give anyone his last dime,
Not just a Dad but a great Friend,
He kept his smile until the end.

He was our Dad and so special,
and that is why this tale I tell.

Greatest of all time (GOAT)

In Men's Tennis, many greats were displayed,
Throughout all the Years that the game has
been played,
Laver, Borg and Sampras are just some,
Of the greats of the game that have come and
gone,
But then there is a new sensation,
Three greats come along in one generation,
Roger, great server with a natural Flair,
Gently caressing the ball through the air,
Floating around like a bird on the breeze,
Playing the game with such utter ease,
Novak the greatest Defender is he,
Returning the serve for him is the key,
Once this player was not so revered,
But now it is he who is the most feared,
Rafa Nadal, king of the clay,
The Greatest Competitor is what they all say,
With great spin and balance, and superfast
feet,
This left handed Houdini never knows when
he's beat,
These Giants win slams like a runaway train,
This great Golden age will not come again,
We each have one that we adore,
That player, the one you always shout for,

But whoever it is that's in your camp,
There is no dispute, they all can be called champ,
Which one of them is the greatest of all,
This question will be asked for evermore,
Many debates over many a beer,
Will rage on and on over the Years,
This Fabulous Three we have been honoured to see,
Are simply the greatest there will ever be,
These Gods of the game have made history,
And will be remembered for eternity.

I Wonder

I wonder why we are all here,
What is it for, is there a purpose,
Or is there no mystery at all,
And it is in fact just one big circus,

It could be that each one as meaning,
And play our part on this chessboard,
Or that each move is merely random,
And no points are ever scored,

We all grow up to believe,
Our destiny's mapped out for us,
Some believe there's an exact time,
When as they say "our numbers up"

One of my theories for all this,
Is all decisions that we make,
Are a new branch, road or direction,
On the Journey that we take,

So in fact could it be,
That there are no actual mistakes,
All are just perhaps experiences,
In creating our final fate,

The Thief of Confidence

I find myself a different Man,
My Confidence where has it gone,
It started to drift away,
When my Father passed away,
Up until then I was so strong,
and so sure for so long,
But since he died it's not the same
It seems someone has changed the game
I then got ill which cost my job
I wonder how I'll earn a bob
The uncertainty in me
Is not something I want to see
But I now see that what I had
Was self belief and my Dad,
With these foundations stripped away,
I'm only Half that Man Today,
I need to fight this sickness fast
Before it gets hold and takes the last
Yes my Father will still be Dead,
But he will never leave my head
And I can rediscover self belief
With Dad onside to fight this thief

Extinct

The world is dying we all know,
No dodo's left or white Rhino,
Many more have left this place,
In the years of Human space,
We hunt or kill their habitat,
With little or no regard for that,

Many at risk, it's so unfair,
Gorilla, Tiger, Polar Bear,
Why won't we stop and stand together,
And change this World back forever,
Otherwise our children will see,
Animals by virtual reality,

There is a blatant disregard,
That we can easily just discard,
So many beautiful species,
And chop down so many trees,
Don't look to Government it's up to us,
The time has come to make a fuss,
And stand together resolute,
We are all responsible so don't be mute,

If we act now there is still time,
although a mountain we have to climb,

All the endangered on that list,
We can ensure they still exist,
We all just need to unite,
Then force the 'others' to see the light,
The time has come to think of others,
The future of our Sisters and Brothers,
And all of those exotic beasts,
Or they will all be deceased,

Morning stroll by the sea

I stand up on the firm wet sand,
The warm sun on my face and hands,
The cool breeze brushing past my side
The sound of the sea, it's endless tide,
The walk upon an autumn beach,
Is not a pleasure one can teach,

seagull cries at break of dawn
Few signs of life in early morn,
Broken shells along the shore,
A stranded Jellyfish I saw,
A few Dogs dart in and out the sea,
But there's little else to hear or see,

For such peace and tranquility,
And to be at one and feel free,
Take a stroll along the sand,
And feel the freedom of this land,
It is a tiny sacrifice,
For such a piece of paradise

Time please Gents

I think it's time now to retire,
It is no longer my desire,
Only smoking ashes where was a fire,
I have to say I do now tire,
Of all I used to tolerate,
No motivation, it is too late,

You see i think I've done my time,
43 years and rarely a sign,
Of gratitude for what I did,
They just wanted me to do their bid,
Not that I mind, I enjoyed my work,
Proud to say I would not shirk,

But now I have just filled the tank,
Time now to empty the bank,
Slow down, relax and just enjoy,
My Family, my pride and joy,
More time to spend just chilling out,
Or getting out and about,

I can go and write poetry,
Sitting down under a tree,
Or play a round of golf or two,
Just doing what I want to do,
Go Horse racing when I like,
A gentle ride out on the bike,

It's getting very tempting now,
All the things I can allow,
A nice hill walk and then an ale,
Okay stop now you've got the sale !
I am convinced it's time to stop
A chance to slow before I drop,

Lots of time to Holiday,
In sunny spots or just get away,
Ireland beckons now much more,
And those nice walks along the shore,
I have to go and make it mine.
Before the big boss up there calls time !

It's a Wonder we can communicate at all

I have studied the English for many a year,
But the more that I study the less that is clear,
So we READ a book but the book is READ,
Which has the same sound as the colour RED,
CHILLY is cold, but CHILLI is hot,
What confusion there is with the language we
got,
We have the river WEAR but we WEAR our
clothes,
And WHERE'S, WHERE we go, oh who
knows,
That PLANE is CLOSE, but the door we
CLOSE,
This is bizarre the words that we chose,
It's PLAIN to see that we got it so wrong,
I can see for miles along a PLAIN so long,
We can WRITE with our pen these words on
a page,
But it won't be RIGHT at any stage,
And RIGHT might be RIGHT but not all the
time,
Because when there is left it's a different sign,
The SUN shines bright up in the AIR,
But the Queens first SON is her HEIR,
And the stuff on your head is your HAIR,
Then there's a large rabbit which is a HARE,

There is a PIER on the beach and we have our
PEERS,
We PEER over the fence at the dashing
DEER,
And oh, my DEAR is fondness for another,
Do your SUM just to please your Mother,
Or SOME detention may come your way,
It is so confusing all these words that we say,
So you can BE okay, but don't get stung by a
BEE,
Two is a PAIR and there is a PEAR tree
You can be naked as Adam and that is BARE,
But that won't give you such a scare,
As a Grizzly BEAR face to face,
He won't hurt a FLY, but you will FLY on
this chase,
THEIR cars are THEIR own,
but THERE are many that AREN'T
Then THERE is THEIR Uncle and THEIR
AUNT,
She SOWS a SEAM or SO it SEEMS,
Rain TEEMS down upon our TEAMS,
WHETHER rain or shine
It's still our WEATHER,
wind BLEW, sky's BLUE,
Like birds of a feather,
two EAR'S that We HEAR with, HERE on
our head,
And I eat my BREAD, I'm so well BRED,

It's made with FLOUR, but not with
FLOWERS,
Mix it up and bake for hours,
I ATE it all up, or I HATE it,
They will bake EIGHT and then they quit,
AYE AYE Captain what can you SEE,
With this one EYE I SEE the SEA,
There's MORE and walk upon the MOOR,
FOR a cricket FOUR and a Golf FORE,
A Lion's ROAR and a vegetable's RAW,
The Eyes SAW, EyeSORE and a woodSAW,
You can lift your leg to climb a STAIR,
But a STARE is a most unwelcome Glare,
Bend down on your knee, PRAY on a pew,
A bird of PREY, others PREY on you,
A Vampires heart thrust a wooden STAKE,
Have a juicy STEAK upon your plate,
Wear a BOW tie smart as a lord,
The actors BOW when the crowd applaud,
Prepare some food, the cheese you GRATE,
GREAT wall of China they did create,
Go to the gym and pump some WEIGHT,
Or WAIT for a bus that will turn up late,
The summer FETE, don't forget the date,
And your destiny is your FATE,
With teenagers GROWN, drink a glass of
WINE,
As nows when they WHINE and GROAN all
the time,
In Autumn, LEAVES fall from the Tree,

And with this last thought I will LEAVE thee,
I think we are talking to the wall,
It's a wonder we can communicate at all !

And for fun there's more
A female sheep is a EWE, but it's not YOU,
There's a HOLE THROUGH the bucket,
But the WHOLE Bucket I THREW,
The sun setting on the sea is a lovely SCENE,
But not so lovely if it's not SEEN,
Rafa will REIGN at Tennis on the Clay
But when it lashes down, RAIN stops play,
Scrooge is as MEAN as he can be,
that MEANS tight, not giving, you see,
these words just CROP up and now revealed,
The Farmers CROP is in the field,
You can TEAR a page or SHED a TEAR,
In the SHED is where you put your SHEARS,
And HIT for the SHEER hell of IT,
PIT your Wits or go down the PIT,
MEET a friend for a dinner and eat some
MEAT,
Run a Marathons a FEAT, but you may have
sore FEET
A SEAL can swim and you can SEAL a leak,
Work all WEEK and you will feel WEAK.
Win that LOT in the auction if you cough
And that's your LOT, I'm signing off !

Dreams

When we close our eyes at Night,
Although asleep we still have sight,
The things that go on in our head,
While lying there within our bed,

Dreams are the name we call that place,
Unconscious mind on interface,
With so many thoughts mixed up in there,
Sorting them out is a nightmare,

Happy Dreams and sad ones too,
Frightening ones are usually few,
We dream a thousand dreams at night,
And yet we usually cannot recite,
A single one we had at all,
It's very strange we can't recall,

Why we dream's a mystery,
Its been theorised through History,
Specialists can now analyse each sort,
Explain what was going on in your thoughts,
I don't think they are for real,
What's in your dreams no one can steal.

We fall asleep and teleport,
To another world is what I thought,
Open a door, your in the sea,

Then proposing on your knee,
Fighting with sword and shield,
Then sunning with friends in a field,

The facts are we will never know,
Why, we have our night time show,
How we can sometimes recall,
And sometimes not at all,
And why most of them make no sense,
Life's mystery or just nonsense ?

Tracks of our Years

When we are young, It happens so slow,
We stay small when we want to grow,
It takes too long to happen we say,
From a simple short journey to a Holiday,
The wait is too long for everything fun,
Birthday, Christmas, a break in the Sun.

Then later we can't wait to leave school,
Get out to work and start being cool,
Girls want to look older by years,
Boys can't wait to be drinking beers,

Now we move on to a later stage,
We have passed our best and we don't want
to age,
Can the years now please slow their pace,
And the lines stop appearing on our face,
It would be nice to start looking younger,
For that, a lot of us now hunger.

But now the years pick up their speed,
They do not give us what we need,
A year goes in the blink of an eye,
So very different now, they fly !
Birthdays and Christmas we don't want to

rush,
But soon enough, they are upon us,

It's funny how life happens this way,
Like the tracks of a record is what I used to
say.
The outside lines are the early years
And that one in the middle is the one that we
fear,
Such long circles when we start out
But much shorter and faster as we come to
bow out

Punk Days

Then came along the Punk Rock scene,
A way to show them what you mean,
Express yourself if you're a teen,
I loved to hear "God save the Queen"
Is it still banned, how longs it been ?
We did rock with hair Blue and Green,

It was a really crazy time,
But to me the music is still so fine,
We were alive and that's the truth,
Perhaps that was just our youth,
On a high with all those gigs,
A bit of blow, booze and some cigs,

A studded nose and earrings,
In those Days were quite shocking,
Crazy colours everywhere,
Or you could have Black Spiked hair ,
There really were no fashion shows
It was just "anything goes" !!

The music was sure something new,
The Clash, The Damned, Sex Pistols too,
Ramones, Devo, Sham 69,
The Undertones and 999,
I know it's one of those cliches,
But it really was "the good old Days"

Our Mom's

We only have one Mom on earth,
So cherish her for all your worth,
No one will ever take her place,
Nothing you do will fill that space,
Of emptiness you feel inside,
When she is taken from your side.

Before you breathe a breath in vain,
She has already suffered pain,
The labour that's the gift of life,
Will cause her pain and stress and strife,
She will suffer much as you grow,
Making sure "the rope you tow".

She will teach you right from wrong,
And morals that will make you strong,
Good manners and etiquette,
Wash the dishes, table set,
She gets you all prepared for school,
You best abide by all those rules.

When you get older and need advice,
She will be there, she won't think twice,
When all the world is against you,
Your Mom's the one who takes your view,
She will stand there and be your rock,
There's not another of that stock,

No one in life will love you more,
But your Mom still knows the score,
Of those who come to steal your heart,
But no one can split you two apart,
So cherish her and hold her tight,
And pray for her most every Night.

The Emerald Isle

This is a place I yearn to be,
I feel it is a part of me,
It was my Fathers Homeland,
And I have to say, it is grand,
The lovely people make you smile,
Oh yes, I love the Emerald Isle,
So proud of my large Family,
The finest people you could see,
Warm and generous and so kind,
A better crowd you could not find,
When I am there I feel so good,
I'm sure that's cause it's in my blood,
So many lovely sights in stock,
Killarney Lakes and Glendalough,
Malahide and the Curragh too,
And that's to name but a few,
Dublin Zoo is inspiring,
A run round Phoenix Park's my thing,
I will soon be back across the sea,
That Emerald Isle is calling me,
One thing to say before I finish,
A pint in Dublin, now that is Guinness.

The Greatest (Ali)

The Greatest, we all knew him well,
This Big man, a tale could tell,
He could have talked his way to fame,
But that was not really his game,
A legend in the boxing Ring,
Now that is what was his thing,

Famous as the former Cassius Clay,
The Canvass was where Liston lay,
When those fast hands did their magic,
And those fast feet, he was so slick,
He changed Heavyweight Boxing,
Champion of the World, they would now
sing,

That was though, just the beginning,
He would have much fun in the ring,
Thriller in Manila was a special one,
The title returned to the number one,
Revenge on Frazier the main foe,
He took a pasting that Day, did Joe,

The Legend had a different Name
Mohammad Ali you can proclaim,
The Fighter was not different though,
Still the same Dance and the same show,
This victory, the deciding fight,

To settle who was best alright,

Now onto the most fearsome man,
George Foreman was now Champion,
A giant who could slay them all,
He threw that right, and they did fall,
There simply was not anyway,
That Mohammed could win that Day,

He won the battle of words though,
And told Foreman what round he'd go,
Everyone thought it was a joke,
No way could Ali drop this big bloke,
But as sure as the grass is green,
He somehow achieved that Dream,

He danced around Big George all night,
George got so tired he could not fight,
Ali would now take control,
He destroyed George's very soul,
In round eight Ali knocked him out,
No one thought he had a shout,

He floated like a butterfly,
And he could talk, he was not shy,
No modesty was not his thing,
But like a bee, he could sting,
The Heavyweight scene is not the same,
Since this legend left the game.

Betrayed

I considered that the Company,
Had thought of me as Family,
But the moment that I got sick,
They thought let's just get rid of quick,
It was just all a great big lie,
They couldn't care if I live or die,
This job that I had done so well,
Didn't matter now "just go to Hell"!
Conscientious and honest,
and always tried to give my best,
Their reward for this was just the sack,
A mighty stab right in the back,
I could not feel more betrayed,
Oh my God, had 1 been played,
They said I was thought of as a Friend,
A Christmas card I will not send,
I'm glad I'm not an enemy,
I dare not think how that would be.

The Country Runner

I have spent my life on the run,
but not from the Police, just for the fun,
and for fitness and good health,
It also helps my mental self,
Sometimes alone, sometimes with friends,
Whom with, many great times I spend,
It's always been a nice escape,
Out there on that great landscape,
The freedom that I find still,
Out there on those fields and hills
Far from that polluting air,
And all those noisy cars down there,
Just the quiet natural sound,
Of tweeting Birds are all around,
Whatever Weather I'm still out there,
Come rain or shine, I don't care,
It is a drug I cannot quit,
When unwell, still need that hit,
Non-runners do not understand,
We are a very special band,
Yes we all know we are quite mad,
This sport for us was not a fad,
The run is done I'm back in,
Recharged, full of Adrenaline,
Always enjoyed, never a chore,
Ready to join the world once more

Lucky me

To even be born at all,
Is an incredible miracle,
Just consider the odds of that,
It is a quite amazing stat,
And then to be born in good Health
A Family of love and wealth
Born into Western civilisation,
It could have been Third World starvation,
Or ravaged War torn Countries,
We would have been poor refugees,
So when we reflect on our own lives,
Remember we are the lucky guys,
We have all won the Lottery,
If well and safe and fed and free,
And please think of the ones that aren't
Help if you can because they can't !

The way we live our lives

We live our lives in different ways,
Ideas of how to spend our Days,
Some afraid to take a chance,
Other's where risk is their stance,
Most are somewhere in between,
A balanced risk is the mean,
A bungy jump gives some a high,
Or Parachute jump from the sky,
Others can be happy in a book,
Or with a fish caught on a hook,
Then there are the keep fit crew,
And those who love the TV view,
Many of us love our sports,
Playing, watching, there are all sorts,
A lot think shopping's fun as well,
Most are female, if truth I tell,
Some think that work is where it's at,
And cannot see much beyond that,
A few of us just love a Beer,
And most of us love Families near,
Whatever it is that makes you tick,
That you enjoy, gives you a kick,
Just try and keep on doing it,
It may improve your life a bit,
If none of this does the trick,
Then get out there and change it quick

Time

If all we get is time and time IS all we get,
We need to make the most of every bit, you
bet !
Some of us will be rich and get a huge
amount,
But this won't mean a thing if we don't make
it count,
And some get a raw deal, are not long for this
world,
But if they can smile and bring some joy, then
their's will be well served,
It is a gift we're given and no one knows how
long,
We each choose how to use it, there is no
right or wrong,

It cannot be bought with wealth or stolen from
someone,
It ours to use how we see and when it's gone,
it's gone,
So don't be wasteful with it and treasure
every Day,
When head is on that pillow, Tomorrow's
ours we pray,

Smile if you can do, and try to laugh too,

But share some thought for others, not as
fortunate as you,
The Memories that we share are the
investments we have made,
With some of that lovely time, that has been
so well repaid,

So you can count your money up, but you're
still on the clock
And you can count your time down,
Tick tock, tick tock, tick tock,
But better to enjoy it, for every single minute,
unlike your bank account, you can't see
what's left in it !

The New Normal

So this is it, it's hard to take,
Curfews, Lockdown, firebreak,
It follows on from Hands, Face, space,
Covid tests and track and trace.

What comes next ? A question pose ?
How we cope ? No one knows,
Is this the new "normal" life ?
Discontent is now rife,

It seems that no one understands,
Such extreme measures in this land,
Not just here, these rules are global,
But this i fear is no Chernobyl !

So if this virus stays with us,
Because the scientists cannot suss,
And so no vaccine can be found,
With more restrictions will we be bound ?

It seems there's now a lot of fear,
Some afraid of coming near,
Afraid of catching Covid-19,
Like it's the worst thing ever seen,

Others scared of loneliness,
Not socialising, phobias,

Mental illness, depression,
No Doctor visits, what's going on ?

Many feel their liberty,
Has been removed, no longer free,
That restrictions have gone too far,
They no longer know who they are.

One things for sure the Country's split,
Perhaps the whole world's been hit,
With exactly the same derision,
Whatever else it feels like prison,

I don't know what the answer is,
Because I am no scientist,
And I'm definitely no clever MP
Although one of them I rarely see

But Hospital ops have all but ceased,
GP appointments have decreased,
And then only as a phone call,
So what's to happen to us all ?

So if you are Ill or need treatment,
You might as well apply ointment,
Or maybe just take a pill,
If it's severe just write your will !

Weather or not

The Weather is so wonderful,
It's Dark and bright and colourful,
Jack frost runs across the grass,
Ice on the paths is just like glass,

The white of snow upon the ground,
The lightning then the crashing sound,
Of Thunder as the skies collide,
The lashing rain the roaring tide,

So suddenly it turns to hail,
Pebbles of ice will now prevail,
Then there's a cool and gentle breeze,
A raging wind downs strongest trees,
The sky is clear, the wind is still
The Sun is warm, no more a chill,
On the horizon a coloured arc,
The rainbow leaves a lasting mark.

The Weather, so many moods it knows,
Angry, unhappy, calm, it shows,
Sometimes just one by one displayed,
And other times all cards are played.

Old Men

The hair goes grey or goes away,
The teeth fall out or gums recede,
The joints all ache or stiffen up,
It's not all fun I can concede,

The bellies grow and muscles waste,
Popping pills, but not for fun,
At the loo half of the night,
And up before the Morning Sun,

Can't go anywhere with out those specs,
But can't remember where they are,
Started liking fawn and beige clothes,
And prefer to drive a slow car !

But now to all of the pluses,
There is free transport on the buses,
The tax man Cannot take that cash,
Have tucked away that tax-free stash,

There is no mortgage anymore,
And now much more time to think,
And how it is to know much more,
And don't live life on the brink,

Moan and groan if you want,
It's allowed when you are old,
if people don't like what you say,

It's not a problem, you are more bold,

Life is looked at differently,
But there is still plenty to enjoy,
No more work and no more stress,
Just like when you were a little Boy !

Then comes a Revolution

I think a revolution's coming,
You cannot lock them up inside,
And destroy their livelihoods,
The nation's eyes are now open wide,
The pressure is now turning up,
The relief valves are all on overload,
I don't think it will take much more,
Before the people explode

In the North they hit them hard,
This part of land already scarred,
With unemployment and poverty,
This is an inequality,
But in the South it's different see,
Because that's where all the wealthy be,
The rules for them don't change that much,
The chosen few they don't even touch,

Back to the point, we need to live,
To see our Friends, and Family,
The current way is not a life,
Our Grand Children we cannot see !
A drink with Friends, a Holiday,
A Family day to celebrate,
It is all just getting worse,
Soon there will be a curfew at Eight,

I wonder what our ancestors would think,
Our freedom has been stripped away,
They dealt with Wars and fatal disease,
It would not have happened in their Day,
They shrugged their shoulders and carried on,
With basic liberties preserved,
Many people lost their lives,
Just so that freedom was served,

Do we let the dictators prevail ?
Or make that call before too late,
It's up to each and everyone,
It's time to decide your own fate,
No one can do it on their own,
But if you can all now unite,
Your freedom is the greatest prize,
And you can still win this fight!

One Flew Over

They want to take complete control,
Steal the fire from inside my soul,
They say that I will not conform,
Just because I won't perform
like a puppet to all their rules,
I am not one of those fools !

One flew over the Cuckoo's nest,
And some of us still know what's best,
There are a few within this nest,
That won't submit like all the rest,
And don't judge us as the bad guys,
This is a ruse, a pack of lies

The victors write the History,
So the bad guys are you see,
Just the losers, in every case,
This is the truth we have to face,
Red indian's in a western flick,
German's, Guy Fawkes take your pick,

So though I still have my own mind,
I begin to think I am one of a kind,
Most have now been conditioned well,
Like under the Pied Piper's spell,
They are trapped in a living hell,
But they don't mind, cause they can't tell.

What they don't know cannot hurt them,
But the likes of us they will condemn,
We are the nutter's is what they think,
The cuckoo's nest, the missing link,
Psychologist I am not,
But the others are the white coat lot !

The Peacemakers

Something that's always troubled me,
Is just how violent people can be,
Blessed are the Peacemakers was once said,
Problem is they are always dead,
Long before their time is due,
And that really doesn't ring true,

Abraham Lincoln was a good man,
Peace and equality he was a fan,
In abolition of the slave,
He only found an early grave

John Lennon sang of ending war
A pacifist he was for sure,
To be gunned down in the Street,
Was not the end that he should meet,

The great Indian Mahatma Gandhi,
A more peaceful man there could not be,
And yet another violent Act,
To end his life and that's a fact

Another one was Jesus Christ,
Only guilty of peaceful advice,
His reward for being a good friend,
Was crucifixion, a grisly end,

JFK was before his time,
To change this world and stand in line,
Peace and equality this man sought,
A shot to the head, ended this thought,

And then came Martin Luther King,
Peace once more, would this man sing,
And that all men were equal,
But again others wanted to kill,

You see the pattern that keeps showing,
And the violence that keeps growing,
For every good there is a bad,
For every Happy there's also sad, So is this
pattern set to repeat ?
It does seem so bittersweet,
That every time we see bright light,
Someone turns up as dark as night.

The King

He was born a poor boy, lived in
Tennessee,
No one knew then just what he would be,
This Boy with the grin and a handsome
face,
Oh he could sing and he could shake the
place,

The girls went crazy when he got on the
stage,
The Boys they loved him, he was all the
rage,
The sound was fast and loud and wild,
Music previously had been so mild,

The older generation were not impressed,
This young upstart who was hardly
dressed,
He couldn't sing and he flexed his hips,
The TV producers needed to get to grips,

So they banned him from Dancing on
TV with haste,
The cameras couldn't show him down
at the waist,
These killjoys hoped they would stop
this fad,

But there wasn't a chance they must
have been mad,

  This Rock n Roll King was here to stay,
The fire starter of all music we hear
Today,
  Lennon said the King was his motive,
David Bowie said that Elvis did give,
Music a whole new start,
  It was rock n roll that was the heart
Of all major musicians tributes,
Without Elvis it would be ballads in
suits,

So we salute the The King and his peers
too,
Buddy, Eddie Cochran, Gene Vincent
are a few,
Of those great men from this wonderful
time,
When music was born and turned into
wine.

Sport of Kings

Mostly it is inside my mind,
That all these strange poems I do find,
To some I may seem very strange,
Especially cause my poems change,
With such a different range of things,
This ones about "the Sport of Kings"

My favourite racehorse of all time,
I will try and tell it in this rhyme,
It's not an easy thing to do,
Ones that I loved were quite a few,
Anyone who really loves this game,
Will probably say they feel the same,

What can I say, where do I start,
Cue Card, the horse who broke my heart,
When he fell in the Gold Cup,
That day you see he had no luck,
Then Sprinter Sacre reclaimed his prize,
Champion again, tears in my eyes,

The Festivals a special place,
It has produced many an ace,
None finer than Kauto Star,
Or the fantastic Altior,
Dawn Run the Mare who done the double,
Jonjo O'Neil never looked in trouble,

I could carry on with Cheltenham Stories,
But we must look at all racing Glories,
Aintree the home of the greatest race,
Grand National the whole world embrace,
The great Red Rum with three Wins,
And little Tiger Roll closing in,
His Greatest hour may have been taken,
But he'll be back next year, no mistaking,

I couldn't end without a thought,
The priceless Horses that can't be bought,
My favourite was the Dancing Brave,
The Derby stolen from the fave
Electric speed but not that much !
But in the Arc he found his touch,

The fastest Horse there's ever been,
Frankel he was his Trainers dream,
Sadly he was to be his last,
But not a single Horse could pass,
This legend was the final word,
Of Henry Cecil that we heard,

This was just a small account,
Of four legged beasts that jockeys mount,
So many have come and gone,
And many more will come along,
To excite us all who love the turf,
And that thumping sound upon the earth,

Of horses as they race along, Now that's the place where I belong.

Wake up

While we all live life like it's a game,
We barely notice all that pain,
and suffering that's out there,
Just what these people have to bear,
Wake up world and change this fate,
Wake up now before it's too late,

I speak about the Yemen plight,
Children will starve to Death Tonight,
The Western World has closed its door,
And will not fund them anymore,
Wake up, this mountain we can climb,
Wake up now, while there's still time,

So we have cut our Foreign aid,
We have our own issues, we are afraid,
We cannot fund this anymore,
Who sold weapons for this war ?
Wake up World, you are to blame,
Wake up now, for its insane !

Unicef have told us this,
Twelve million kids are at high risk,
dying from starvation or disease,
If this disaster we cannot cease,
Wake up World, Western World,
These Children's fate is undeserved

GB Legends

The two footballers I adored,
Were from an era long ago,
When I was just a small Boy,
But both could put on quite a show,

From very humble beginnings,
And personalities miles apart,
But they really were my boyhood hero's,
And will always be close to my heart,

Different positions on the pitch,
'Greatest' was what they were to me,
strangely they had the same initials,
Those golden letters were GB,

Well now that clue is out the bag,
I'm sure any football fan has guessed,
The Greatest keeper Gordon Banks
And Greatest Player is George Best,

From a time when men were men,
And Footballers were not so rich,
When Football had a real magic,
When Giants like these walked on the pitch,

The Greatest save of all time
From Pele's header's what they say,

And no one on earth, could get that Ball,
From Super Georgie on his Day,

These Players were so very special,
I was blessed to see them in the Flesh,
I tingled when they walked on the Pitch,
They were for sure the very best,

They were a big part of my childhood,
I'm not ashamed to say I cried,
When finally their lives were over,
And those Great Legends sadly died.

And The children ask why ?

A burning desire to get rich,
Leave the starving ones to die,
Money matters so much,
And the Children ask why ?

Fighting wars and killing Men,
Women and Children wave Goodbye,
All in the name of Nation or God
And the Children ask why,

Need that new promotion,
Get to the top, they have to try,
Need a bigger better car,
And the Children ask why ?

Moan about everything,
All just like to whinge and cry,
Can't just enjoy what they have,
And the Children ask why,

We should set the example,
They should be asking how Birds Fly ?
Not who decides who gets what when,
But the Children ask why ?

The Good die young

I'm sitting here writing these rhymes,
As once again a light goes out,
The good ones seem to get less time,
I wonder what life's all about,

All through My Years I've had to say,
to many young friends Goodbye,
The life they seem to get his brief,
So unfair they have to die,

The good die young is often spoke,
As if it's a reward for being nice,
But surely if they live that way,
They should have got their lifetime twice !

The facts are that there are no rules,
Some Stirling folk get a good innings,
But none know what card they're dealt,
Or whether they will get the winnings,

So all you can do is live each Day,
And hope you get another one,
For sure enough the day will come,
When all your winnings will be gone

Jesus Christ

It may just have been a story,
He may not have been Gods Son
But he filled the World with Glory,
With his love, the hearts he won,

A wise man he was for sure,
For he realised this much,
That It is not all about you,
But more the people that you touch

Jesus taught us the path of life,
He taught us we were all equal,
And never judge or segregate,
Because we're all God's People,

Believe in God or don't believe,
It really matters not,
But Living life the rightful way,
Is the message that we got,

So regardless of who we are,
We have all received the word,
The greatest story ever told ?
Or best message ever heard !

It's all in the mind

Inside the mind is where it is,
Every single thing we quiz,
From when we're born the questions pour,
Why ? when ? how ? what ?
We must know more,

With an insatiable need to know,
That just continues as we grow,
And just for a while the urges fall,
In early teens we know it all,

Then we continue on our spree,
To college or university,
Many will take their learning far,
With Doctorate or Professor,

Some continue on their study,
For many now the waters muddy,
Now is the time to question all,
Everything we learnt from when were small,

Religion, Politics,History,
Is it all conspiracy?
Is there much truth in what we read,
Have 'they' just been planting a seed ?

Opinions will change within the best,

We now all face the greatest test,
What is this really all about,
Some higher plan or is there nowt ?

Today's another Day

Each time I wake I have to say,
Thank God I have another Day,
The big man up above as said,
I can get up and out of bed,

The glass is half full is my motto,
We teach our kids this as they grow,
To cherish every Day we get,
And live them all without regret,

We must remember when we moan,
That others out there are alone,
Or unwell, in grief or poverty,
This helps restore reality,

So in the morn when you awake,
Take a little smile, for heavens sake,
And think you pinched another chance,
To show this world just how to dance.

The Secret of Life

Live this life the way you should,
Always try to do some good,
Put your faith in Humankind,
You will be repaid within your mind,

Those who do seek power and wealth,
Are mostly in it for them self,
They do not understand the rules,
Perhaps they are just really fools,

The people who would bear no ill,
Not envious or judgmental,
These are the ones who enjoy life,
Without turmoil and without strife,

The ones who prefer to give,
Be it kindness, help or with,
Compassion or friendship,
These are the ones that make life tick,
They have found the key to it,
We all can too, so please don't quit.

Happiness

It's not a secret or hard to see,
But some people find great difficulty,
Won't be found in material things,
Expensive cars or Diamond rings,

Its not something you can go out and find,
It really is all in your mind,
Some things will help certainly.
Good health, Good Friends and Family.

But happiness is found inside,
And not in envy, ego or pride,
Contentment is part of the key,
and the great outdoors helps for me.

Some will find it in their faith,
Or when they relax or meditate,
We all need companionship too,
A soul mate is good for you,
But in the end our destiny,
Depends on what we want to be.

Big Joe

A great friend for many a Year,
I think of him with a tear,
A giant Man with a giant heart,
You would never have known that at the start.

He was so quiet and so thin,
as a 7 year old, when I first knew him,
Playing Football on the wing
Not right there in the thick of things.

But as he aged he grew and grew,
In body and in mind too,
He was now no longer small
He could go through a brick wall.

On the pitch no one would pass by,
Legally or otherwise,
Big Joe was a lovely guy,
He wouldn't say boo to a fly.

So here is to you my big friend,
We will remember you until the end,
We raise a Guinness to you almost always
and we will meet again one of these Days.

Locked in

They said it was just a flu,
I don't think that was true,
Then they said it spread too fast,
And that it wasn't going to last.

We can do herd immunity,
and get rid of it quickly,
They soon changed their tune,
that this will not leave us soon.

Now you must social distance,
and only talk across a fence,
This then became lock down,
Now you can't go to Town.

The Pubs and cafes must close,
Restaurants and Theatre shows,
all non-essential work and things,
all Leisure Centre's, shops and Gyms.

Now they say, may be more to come,
Might completely take our freedom,
No exercise or go outside,
Mental issues, suicide ?
Hope it doesn't get that bad,
We need to be safe not sad.

Let's clamp down on the minority,
That are threatening our liberty.

A Quiet Land

It is a much quieter land Today,
It's like a Sunday every Day,
Less Cars less buses and less Trains,
The noises that would fill our Brains.

Car stereos bang bang bang,
There's none of that in this land,
Children's playgrounds, silent and eerie,
Where There was always laughing and glee.

No roaring planes up in the sky,
All of those sounds, they did all die,
There are no pubs and shops open,
Where idle chatter would go on.

It seems that we now speak not much,
and it is only to keep in touch,
The Birds still sing up in the Trees,
The streams and Rivers will not cease.

The Sea tide still crashes against the shore,
But there is no ring on your front Door,
I think maybe we use this time,
To reflect and re-align,
and when it changes back again,
We will all be a bit more sane.

Mother Nature

Covid-19, the enemy unseen,
its stolen millions of dreams,
It was in China, in Wuhan,
Where Covid hatched its master plan.

With rapid re-production,
To wipe out human population,
It sent its carriers round the globe,
To infect all with the microbe.

It started with the weak and old,
But then needed more, so took the bold,
Brave Doctors on the frontline,
and then came a deadly sign.

Would it now take healthy and fit ?
and show no signs to wane or quit,
An Insatiable appetite,
to reproduce, we cannot fight.

no vaccine or cure found yet,
If not soon the Earth is set,
for a new phase, a different time,
the Human race is on the line.

Perhaps its Mother Nature's plan,
to punish the wrong ways of man,
for abusing the planet for so long
Has judgement Day came along ?

Or is there hope, we can return,
to the times, that we now yearn,
When folk would all help each other,
anyone, not just their Brother.

Will we respect the land at least,
and tiny birds and largest beasts,
and let our World breathe again,
and maybe then She will stop the pain.

All lives matter

All lives matter, seems to me, to make more
sense,
Before we get on our high horse, let's look at
the evidence,
For once we start to segregate, by Class,
religion, Colour, race,
We have already singled out, which is how
we got into this place.

So all lives matter truth be told,
Black or White, young or old,
Rich or poor, Christian, Muslim,
None of us are without sin.

The simple message should say to all,
Judge not, be not narrow minded or small,
Love our neighbour like our Brother,
Respect all others like our Mother,
Find the best in everyone,
And if you can't then just move on.

If we want to look at the oppressed,
I think we might have failed the test,
In Africa, South America or the Middle East,
People starving and dying, doesn't cease.

These are the minorities in the planet we
walk,
But it seems we're ignoring not willing to
talk,
If it's all going on in third world states,
Seems, it doesn't matter so much mate!

This is the clearest case of discrimination,
But so busy moaning, we can't see this
creation.
We need to join ranks for the good,
And make the world our neighbourhood,

Even out the disproportion,
We all need to share our own good fortune,
Then truly we can close the book,
And give this World an equal look.

The Mask Dilemma

The mask dilemma let me explain,
I don't claim to have a super brain,
But it appears simple to me,
Please read and see if you agree,
The mask protects the wearer not,
Any of the others, yes the lot,
So wear a mask upon your face,
And banish Covid from this place,
An easy sum that starts will nil,
Nil times nil, times nil, don't kill.

This I suggested back in March,
When Covid was on its March,
But they thought a mask would do no good,
I don't think that they understood,

And so, 4 Months on we're in July,
So now they say that we will try,
To wear the masks we didn't need,
But now we do, are they on weed ?
They would not protect us when Thousands dying,
But they do now, is someone lying,

The Virus is now in remission,
So wear the masks is there decision,
Well there you have it, crystal clear,

It has all been done to create fear,
And keep the "control thing" rolling on,
What will they do when it has gone,

I'm sure we'll get the second wave,
So please just make sure you save,
Your mask, for when it subsides again,
They will say that we need to regain,
Our masks and wear them on our face,
Until we completely banish from this place,

I sometimes think I'm going mad,
Maybe not, but it does seem bad,
They play with us as if we're fools,
Wear your mask, don't break the rules,
If you do, no shops or Trains,
And we will fine you for your pains,
Yes it's all a crazy Dream
I will wake up soon and scream !

Jobsworth

Grow up and get a job,
Was the way we learnt to earn a bob,
That is how it used to be,
That's how my folks told it to me,

You need to work to pay your keep.
So get out there and not a peep,
It doesn't matter what you do,
Just earn enough to get you through,

We learnt quick to stand on our feet,
If not we might be on the street,
It wasn't bad to learn this truth,
The Parents can't support the youth,

Just take one piece of advice on it,
Which will ensure you do not quit,
Pick something that you love to do,
Then it won't feel like work to you,

Nowadays, it's changed a bit,
Parents can help support with it,
They have more money and more time,
To help their youngsters down this line,

The kids they get to choose their field,
And all the money it may yield,

They get support from Parents too,
don't usually have to pay their due,

But even now with this you see,
It still can turn out not to be,
For if they choose just for Money,
It may not be the Milk and Honey.

It's life Jim, but not as we know it !

Orphiuchus, is the new star sign,
So it was nonsense all the time,
So even if you did believe it,
It's a fact it was real bull-shit
Just proving once again,
Nothing in this life stays the same,
So from a ram to a fish,
I really didn't expect this !

Next they will say Elvis is not dead, JFK did
not get shot in the head,
Teenage kicks not a great tune,
That people walked on the Moon,
That Donald Trumps a bad Guy,
And even that pigs can't fly,
I'm unsure now, it seems surreal,
I'm getting confused with what is real,

If everything we thought we knew,
Is it turns out, totally untrue,
It's very easy now to see,
That we don't know who are we ?
Like Dr McCoy said despondently
In the Star Trek world of reality,
"It's life Jim but not as we know it"
I think perfectly, that this does fit.

Free will

The trouble with the World Today,
Is that we all have the right to say,
We have freedom to speak what we think,
But if not the popular thought you stink.

So in a World where we have freedom,
To speak out, cannot be done,
Or you will be singled out,
made to appear a rebellious lout.

So just be quiet and keep mouth closed,
And you will be home and hosed,
Popular and loved by all,
Your thoughts are locked behind a wall,
A prison cell is what you find,
With bars blocking what's on your mind,

That's not for me, it seems like hell,
Always ashamed, afraid to tell,
What you think shows on your face,
You know how you could change this place,

With debate and discussion,
You might change their opinion,
Or make them all realise,
What's staring them right in the eye's,

That conditioning starts with Government,
Then Companies with advertisement,
The media play the biggest hand,
In trying to rule in this land,
With carefully selected crap,
That is how they lay their trap.

And now supported by social sites,
Gullible volunteers to spread this shite,
I wonder where it all will end,
Will we all just go round the bend ?

The Duel

There came a time in history,
Two exceptional runners were to be,
In constant battle for the glory,
This is how I recount their story,

Middle distance was their speciality,
In both distances a great rivalry,
800 was supposed to be Seb's best,
And the 1500 was Steve Ovett's,

It didn't quite work out that way,
In Moscow Olympics on that Day,
Steve Ovett favourite for the metric mile,
But it was Seb Coe's glory, he did it in style.
His turn of foot was quite supreme
a winners medal more than he dreamed,

They lined up for the Eight hundred race,
Seb it seemed, would have too much pace,
But Steve Ovett would not fold,
It was he who would strike first for Gold,
Steve had swooped as Seb had snoozed,
It was Steve's to win, not Sebs to lose.

During this golden spell of runs,
They broke world records just for fun,

Seb had four at once on the track,
But Steve was there to take them back,
Eighteen World records they set all told,
Coe set twelve, six Ovett did hold,
A special time, their rivalry,
To see again is unlikely.

Working Class Heroes

It was 30th July In Sixty six,
Eleven lads walked on that pitch,
They didn't realise that Day,
That victory would mean more Today,
Than it even meant back then,
We wouldn't win that cup again

These unassuming modest guys,
To see Today it would surprise,
Players are now paid far too much,
Passionless and out of touch,
With the fans who pay their wage,
They dance around like they're on stage,
No longer is this a man's game,
And that is really such a shame,
They all now have such big egos,
Worlds apart from our Heroes,

So let's get back to that subject,
The superstars who won that cup,
They all earned a thousand pounds for that,
An eye they didn't even bat,
For that money meant nothing,
Winning for them was everything,

The point I think I want to say,
Is that the Footballers Today,

We should not even mention them,
In the same breath as these great Men,
Would they even put on the Jersey,
If they had to do it for free?
In the past a cap they got,
That wouldn't work with this lot,

The working class heroes of that time,
Were a special crop, so sublime,
The reason we won the cup that Day,
Was because of great team play,
Great spirit and great talent too,
World class players shining through,

These great men were so humble,
Not the kind that moan and grumble,
Winning for them was not a fluke,
In that time they were the best group,

We will not recreate this feat
It's not something we can repeat,
Not only do we lack the skill,
Our Boys Today don't have the will,
They're all too aloof and so vain,
It's all down to what they can gain,

Strange the Germans won so much,
I never think that they lost touch,
With teamwork and the fatherland,
They simply are a different brand,

For them their Country and their pride,
That's why always an awesome side,
In Sixty Six we had our one taste,
Our faith in them was not misplaced,
Working class heroes did us proud,
These Players put us on a cloud.

Smile

It is so hard sometimes to smile,
But it's even harder still to cry,
They say more muscles used to frown,
So it sure is better to at least try,

A smile will bring joy to others,
And supposedly it's contagious,
So the more that we smile each Day,
The more that others smile at us.

Apparently it helps our health,
To look at life more happily,
If we smile and laugh a little more,
This life will be filled with more glee,

In summary if we can smile,
Even when we don't feel we could,
Others will smile back at us,
that simple act will make us all feel good !

Pain

Living with pain is so very hard,
Others you see cannot understand,
When you are finding it hard to just
concentrate,
The agony that you have to withstand.

You find that it consumes your life,
You lose interest in everything,
Your closest friends think you're depressed,
When you don't answer when they ring.

You are locked out of the real World,
No cure from your suffering,
Hypochondriac is what they think,
When Doctors tests, no answers bring.

Now you feel even more alone,
Your Friends and Family now relieved,
No Terminal illness can be found,
But now you are even less believed.

The trap that you find yourself caught in,
Is that the Doctors do lose interest,
They have checked all the obvious signs,
So they just see you as a pest,

So where can you go from here,
No medication and no cure,

The only hope that now is left,

The Gayle Force

Ninety one at Wembley,
What a sight we were to see,
Little did we know that Day,
What a game he was to play,

Blues v Tranmere was the Game,
Leyland Daf the Trophy name,
Macari was the man in the seat,
John Gayle, the world at his feet,

We started well and took the lead,
And Big John was the feed,
Nodded on with Sturridge set,
The ball was soon in the net,

Then the Gayle force did start,
To break all those Tranmere Hearts,
A step over and a thunderous shot,
We were up two nil and looking hot,

Second half a different story,
Rovers still chasing glory,
Came racing back, goals on cue,
It was now Tranmere turning the screw,

Now only one team could win,
All our nerves were wearing thin,

And then from out of the Blue,
We could not believe it was true,

A late free kick was floated in,
Nodded back and then the spin,
Johnny Gayle getting set,
Wonder goal in the net,

Blues fan jubilant and very loud,
We could not believe it in the crowd,
An overhead kick all skill no luck,
We had just won that cup,

The Gayle Storm was not seen again,
But that Day, I can make this claim,
He was good as any on that show
A legend always, for me though.

Printed in Great Britain
by Amazon

51606355R00047